ANIMAL SAFARI

Snow Leopards

by Megan Borgert-Spaniol

BELLWETHER MEDIA · MINNEAPOLIS, MN

Note to Librarians, Teachers, and Parents:

Blastoff! Readers are carefully developed by literacy experts and combine standards-based content with developmentally appropriate text.

Level 1 provides the most support through repetition of high-frequency words, light text, predictable sentence patterns, and strong visual support.

Level 2 offers early readers a bit more challenge through varied simple sentences, increased text load, and less repetition of high-frequency words.

Level 3 advances early-fluent readers toward fluency through increased text and concept load, less reliance on visuals, longer sentences, and more literary language.

Level 4 builds reading stamina by providing more text per page, increased use of punctuation, greater variation in sentence patterns, and increasingly challenging vocabulary.

Level 5 encourages children to move from "learning to read" to "reading to learn" by providing even more text, varied writing styles, and less familiar topics.

Whichever book is right for your reader, Blastoff! Readers are the perfect books to build confidence and encourage a love of reading that will last a lifetime!

This edition first published in 2014 by Bellwether Media, Inc.

No part of this publication may be reproduced in whole or in part without written permission of the publisher. For information regarding permission, write to Bellwether Media, Inc., Attention: Permissions Department, 5357 Penn Avenue South, Minneapolis, MN 55419.

Library of Congress Cataloging-in-Publication Data

Borgert-Spaniol, Megan, 1989- author.
  Snow Leopards / by Megan Borgert-Spaniol.
    pages cm. – (Blastoff! Readers. Animal Safari)
  Summary: "Developed by literacy experts for students in kindergarten through grade three, this book introduces snow leopards to young readers through leveled text and related photos"– Provided by publisher.
  Audience: 5 to 8.
  Audience: K to grade 3.
  Includes bibliographical references and index.
  ISBN 978-1-60014-968-9 (hardcover : alk. paper)
  1. Snow leopard–Juvenile literature. I. Title. II. Series: Blastoff! readers. 1, Animal safari.
  QL737.C23B6694 2014
  599.75'55–dc23
                                                    2014000107

Printed in the United States of America, North Mankato, MN.

Contents

What Are Snow Leopards?

Snow leopards are **big cats**. They live high up on mountains.

Their fur is light with dark circles. It is thick to keep them warm in winter.

Snow leopards have large paws. They can walk on top of deep snow.

Snow leopards also jump and climb. Their long tails help them **balance**.

Hunting and Eating

Snow leopards **stalk** sheep, goats, and other **prey**.

Then they **pounce**. They can leap as far as 50 feet (15 meters)!

A snow leopard takes several days to eat its meal. It protects its kill from **scavengers**.

Cubs

A female snow leopard has two or three **cubs**. They stay safe in a **den**.

The cubs learn
how to hunt at
3 months old.
The chase is on!

Glossary

balance—to stay steady and not fall

big cats—large wild cats; lions, tigers, and leopards are all big cats.

cubs—young snow leopards

den—a shelter for wild animals; snow leopards make dens between large rocks.

pounce—to leap on top of something

prey—animals that are hunted by other animals for food

scavengers—animals that feed on the meat of dead animals

stalk—to secretly follow

To Learn More

AT THE LIBRARY

Borgert-Spaniol, Megan. *Leopards*.
Minneapolis, Minn.: Bellwether Media, 2013.

Esbaum, Jill. *Snow Leopards*. Washington,
D.C.: National Geographic, 2014.

Kurkov, Lisa. *Roar! Big Cats*. Greensboro,
N.C.: Carson-Dellosa, 2014.

ON THE WEB

Learning more about
snow leopards is as easy as 1, 2, 3.

1. Go to www.factsurfer.com.

2. Enter "snow leopards" into the search box.

3. Click the "Surf" button and you will see a
   list of related web sites.

With factsurfer.com, finding more information
is just a click away.

Index

The images in this book are reproduced through the courtesy of: Bildagentur Zoonar GmbH, front cover; Mikael Males, p. 5; Stayer, p. 7; FLPA/ SuperStock, p. 9; Jeannette Katzir Photog, p. 11; Andy Poole, p. 13 (top); Klesz, p. 13 (bottom left); USBFCO, p. 13 (bottom right); Gerard Lacz Images/ SuperStock, p. 15; CRG Photo/ Alamy, p. 17; David & Micha Sheldon/ F1 Online/ SuperStock, p. 19; Purple Pilchards/ Alamy, p. 21.